Introduction

Most people are not aware of the significance of Vastu Shastra in their daily lives, nor do they understand how it affects their homes and offices. Vastu Shastra has a long history of working with the natural energies that surround us on a daily basis, and now we can learn how to use these energies to improve our lives, our health, and our relationships. Using color, style, materials, positioning, and decorations a person can not only control the flow of energy in their environment with positive results, they can also increase their own energy levels and experience better mental and physical health.

The point of Vastu Shastra is to arrange your home and work spaces in a way that mimics nature to allow for the advantages of the life force energies and limit the energies that impact in negative ways. Vastu Shastra teaches that everything is joined through energy, and therefore even your thoughts and conduct can be impacted by your environment.

Vastu, yoga, and Ayurveda are interrelated branches of Vedic knowledge that speaks about human life and the whole universe. Vastu is Indian/Vedic Feng Shui. Vastu Shastra is a part of this ancient knowledge base. This book seeks to bring you a basic understanding of the ways in which you can use

COPYRIGHT © 2016 BY MICHAEL DINURI. ALL RIGHTS RESERVED

This document is geared towards providing exact and reliable information in regards to the topic and issue covered. The publication is sold with the idea that the publisher is not required to render accounting, officially permitted, or otherwise, qualified services. If advice is necessary, legal or professional, a practiced individual in the profession should be ordered.

- From a Declaration of Principles which was accepted and approved equally by a Committee of the American Bar Association and a Committee of Publishers and Associations.

In no way is it legal to reproduce, duplicate, or transmit any part of this document in either electronic means or in printed format. Recording of this publication is strictly prohibited and any storage of this document is not allowed unless with written permission from the publisher. All rights reserved.

Table of Contents

Introduction 1

Chapter 1: Vastu Shastra—Ancient Science for Modern Times 3

Chapter 2: The Universal Life Force 15

Chapter 3: Bedrooms 27

Chapter 4: Other Rooms and Areas of the Home 35

Chapter 5: Cleaning to Improve Vastu Energies 47

Chapter 6: The Yard and Garden 53

Chapter 7: Improve and Increase Personal Prana 57

Conclusion 65

About the Author 67

this ancient knowledge in today's modern world in terms that are easy to understand with ideas that are easy to follow. Even though the concept is from ancient times, the flow of energy that surrounds us is timeless, and therefore will never cease to exist. So in order to work with these energies and to improve our own lives, it is a wise thing to undertake learning how to harness the power of these energies to make ourselves whole in mind and body and more in tune with the energies of the universe.

Chapter 1: Vastu Shastra—Ancient Science for Modern Times

Vastu Shastra (*vāstu śāstra*) is traditionally an ancient Indian Vedic system of architecture. The architectural designs are intended to integrate building designs with nature, the relative functions of various parts of a building, and ancient beliefs utilizing geometric patterns, symmetry, and specific alignments.

Vastu Shastra is part of the *Vastu Vidya*, which is an older manuscript about architecture and design theories from ancient India. *Vastu Vidya* is a collection of ideas and concepts which is not rigid, but instead is a model for the organization of space within a building based on the space's usage.

The Sanskrit word *Vastu* means "the site or foundation of a house, building, dwelling place, habitation, or house." The root word *vas* means "to dwell, live, stay, or reside." The term *Shastra* has been translated to mean "doctrine or teaching." Therefore, *Vastu Shastra* literally means "the science of dwellings" and it is the manual of architecture which contains *Vastu Vidya*, or the knowledge of dwellings.

Known Buildings

Historians have determined that Vastu Shastra was developed between 6000 BCE and 3000 BCE. Even though the principles seem ancient by our modern standards, many well-known temples still stand that have used these building principles. The Iraivan Temple in Hawaii in the United States (built in modern times) and the Angkor Wat Cambodian Temple (which is one of the world's largest ancient Hindu Temples), the Taj Mahal of India, and the Mayan pyramids clearly shows the same architectural designs that are described in the ancient Indian Vastu Shastra's manuals. Ancient India produced many Vastu Shastra manuals mostly for Hindu Temple layouts with many of the manuals including designs for houses and entire villages.

These designs included not only buildings, but also bodies of water and gardens designed to achieve harmony with nature. The ancient Vastu Shastra texts describe the relations and adjustable layouts for rooms or buildings, but did not mandate a set order of architecture. The basic theme is around core elements of a central space, the peripheral zones, direction of windows and doors with respect to sunlight and moon light, and the functions of the rooms involved.

Excavations for the old high culture cities of Harappa and Mohenjodaro, on the Indus River in northwestern India, show how Vastu was used for city planning and buildings. In the great Indian epics there is mention of Vastu Shastra several times in the Mahabharata and the Ramayana which describes how tall royal buildings such as Mount Kailash were built, and whole cities, such as the well-known city of Ayodhya, which is known as Lord Rama's city in the Ramayana, was built according to Vastu Shastra. Another incident from the Mahabharata tells the story of when Lord Krishna built his kingdom, Dwarka, according to Vastu principles. Lord Krishna claimed that when his life was done here on earth, the city would sink into the sea. The remnants of the town of Dwarka have recently been discovered in the Arabian Sea.

Mamuni Mayan

Of the numerous Sanskrit records mentioned in ancient Indian literature, only a few have been translated into English. Many manuscripts include chapters on architecture for temples, homes, villages, streets, shops, public wells, public bathing houses, public gathering halls, gardens, river fronts, and other things. In some cases, parts of the manuscripts are lost and some are available only in Tibetan, Nepalese, or South Indian languages. Other original Sanskrit manuscripts are available only in parts of India. Ancient texts point to the origination of Vastu with a man named Mamuni Mayan. Mayan lived to the south of India around 10,000 BCE when his knowledge of sacred architecture was spread by way of his travels and those of his students when they journeyed across the ocean. Merchants that traveled along trade routes brought back more than medicine, spices, and treasures when they traveled from India to Europe as records show that India's Vedic traditions were also passed on this way. Greece and Rome also have a history record of receiving information in this same manner.

Vastu Purusha Mandala

The written records report that buildings set to the grid patterns of Vastu principles by divine or natural law creates buildings that are alive, nourishing, and supportive, which translates into better health for the people that live within such structures. At the most basic design level, Vastu buildings are based on the principle of Vastu Purusha Mandala, which is often described as the diagram of the universe in miniature. While based on a system of using a grid pattern, it is more than just a simple set of squares.

In Sanskrit, *mandala* means circle. Mandalas are archetypal images found in nature and art that are a type of sacred geometry of cosmic diagram that gives reference to what exists on a level of reality that we normally do not perceive. All mandalas radiate from a center point in a balanced manner in all directions. This structure is related to creation, pure energy, or pure consciousness as it enters the world through a center point and radiates out as a physical manifestation.

Purusha is described as a mythological being that had to be restrained by the gods, who ended up sitting on top of him in order to rehabilitate him. This represents creating order. Purusha is also described as the cosmic man, the universal self, the masculine divine, or pure consciousness. He is pictured face down in a grid of squares to represent his union with Earth Mother, or Prakriti, who is the supporter of our day-to-day existence as humans on this earth.

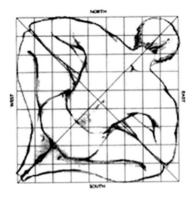

The Vastu Purusha Mandala shows the union of the masculine and the feminine sides of nature at the divine level while the reality remains that both cosmic and earth energies are equal and without gender differences. What it does promote is a healthy balance that is lively and whole so that the deepest level of self is based in nature. A home based on Vastu therefore provides us with a shelter that enlivens our consciousness, supports nature, and becomes a fountain of joy from which we can draw unlimited wellness from. Vastu principles are scientifically based and use the mechanics of nature to transform energy into matter so that both work together. The grid patterns of the Vastu Purusha Mandala create a healthy and energetic effect within the structure that is built according to its guidelines.

Vastu Shastra in India—Journey into Modern Times

If we look at India's long history, much has happened to keep the Vedic tradition from being wiped out completely when other cults and religions became integrated into the country. When Buddhism began to gain a foothold and started propagating across the country, Hinduism and Vedic cultural beliefs were threatened to be lost until a known champion, Adi Shankara, gave new strength to the doctrines and restored the Vedic way of thinking.

The Muslim conquest that began in the 1200s came as the next big threat to the Vedic tradition and over time comingled and integrated with India's culture. Not only did they bring a new religion, but they also brought new architectural designs that later mixed with the Indian architecture which led to great monuments like the Taj Mahal that was built by Mughal emperor Shah Jahan for his beloved wife, Mumtaz. Construction started in 1632 and was completed around 1643. Many architects were involved in the work of the Taj Mahal and the entire structure was built according to Vastu principles.

Finally, when peace and unity began to prevail and the Vedic tradition began to flourish again in the 1700s, the next big threat came when the British began to conquer India. This caused a huge effect not only on the country and the people, but also to the many thousand-year-old culture and heritage. The British considered other cultures and religions that were not advocating Christianity as pagan and many prohibitions followed. The British did not allow or tolerate the beliefs many Indians followed, including: Ayurveda, yoga, and Vastu. During the British colonial period, which ended in 1947 when India became independent, Vastu knowledge almost disappeared completely. During the '80s a few entrepreneurs in Southern India began using Vastu to make changes to their industrial buildings after their businesses experienced substantial losses. When their businesses began to make huge profits, there was an about-face in attitudes about Vastu knowledge which paved the way for the rebirth of Vastu Shastra.

Something happened in recent times and people started to show strong interest in the topic. Old antique books were picked up and many new books on the old practices of Vastu, Ayurveda, and yoga were written. Thanks to the media, Vastu became a hot topic during the '90s. Western civilization now embraces yoga, Ayurveda, and Vastu as a normal way of life.

The principles of Vastu Shastra is witnessing a major revival and wide usage in the planning of individual homes, complexes, commercial and industrial buildings, and other major public building projects in India. While skeptics still scoff at such ancient techniques, scientific studies are prompting people to take a closer look at how they organize their homes to maximize natural benefits from the external environment.

While it is not always practical to rebuild or even remodel your residence or work place, it is possible to make smaller changes to the internal environment that are more in line with Vastu Shastra standards and still provide benefits both physically and mentally from the environment in which you live. The main focus of this book will be to help you find the areas in your home or work spaces where you can make these changes. If you are in a position to be able to build a home or workshop to actual Vastu Shastra standards, or you can make corrections to a home that is already built, it would be advisable to seek out the recommendations of a professional in the field of Vastu Shastra. This book is for the general improvement of Vastu in your home and work space.

Because most people already have a home they are living in and are seeking ways to improve the environment within their homes, I will focus on improvements rather than the building of a perfect home by Vastu Shastra standards. Because of the highly scientific nature of building by Vastu Shastra standards, I would advise a person seeking to build a new home to get in touch with a professional in the field who can provide step-by-step guidance.

Homes obviously come in many shapes and sizes, from the small loft-style efficiency apartments to multi-roomed mansions. I will therefore try to cover the most common rooms in an average-sized house. In general, interior decorating of any house is based on creating positive zones to offset the effects of any negative areas within your structure. Much like the Chinese design system of Feng Shui (which translates as wind and water) the idea is to build spaces that do not obstruct the flow of the universal life energy (which is called *prana* in Sanskrit) to enable optimal beneficial results in the life and health of the occupants of the home or other buildings.

Therefore, according to Vastu Shastra standards, less positive energy zones are usually located in the south, west, and southwestern corners of rooms and this is where heavy furniture and large decorative objects should be located. The positive areas in the north, east, and northeastern corners are where you would place light furniture and small uplifting decorative objects.

Chapter 2: The Universal Life Force

The knowledge of Vastu Shastra has been recorded in several ancient Vedic texts, and is a large and important part of the Indian millennia-old culture in the same way as yoga, Ayurveda, and astrology. Veda is full and pure knowledge, and it is said that it was conveyed when the material world was created trillions of years ago. The purpose of the Vedas is that it tells us about our need to develop as a whole person, both physically and spiritually, to realize that spirit and matter are not separate from each other and they are different parts of the same reality. Many parts of the Vedic texts describe how we can achieve both material success as well as spiritual. Therefore, we are spiritual beings who have a temporary physical form to experience the material world and everything is first created in the spirit, which then takes physical form in the three-dimensional world that we perceive through our five human senses.

Prana is a Sanskrit word which means subtle, universal life-force energy. Feng Shui and other Oriental medicines would call this energy force "chi." The idea is that this energy is essential to every living creature and flows through the entire universe which creates a bond between all living things, planets, atoms, and the universe itself. All creation is created by this life-force energy, is kept alive by it, and then when it ceases to exist as an individual creation, it rejoins the universal prana. As individuals, we use this prana for our daily existence and do not even recognize its influences on our bodies, minds, or our life activities.

Vastu Shastra teaches there are unperceivable energy lines that encompass the Earth, running from north to south and east to west. The electromagnetic fields along these lines influence the human body at the cellular level and affect the organs of the body. Because of this understanding of electromagnetic fields, it is also understood that physical structures will cause breaks in the flow of prana. Vastu Shastra helps us restore the harmony with the natural flow of prana both through and around our homes and other structures. When this harmony is reestablished, the structures vibrate amicably with the universe and these vibrations influence the people of the home by creating a peaceful, happy, and successful atmosphere within the home and their lives.

Panchabhutas: The Five Elements

A key principle of Vastu is that everything is connected through energy. This means that your thoughts and feelings, even your behavior, are strongly influenced by your surroundings. In Vastu, each direction of the home is influenced by a particular energy.

The universe is nature's perfect and beautiful creation where all the matter that the universe is built from is from five basic and essential elements. The world's most famous equation shaped by Albert Einstein, $E = mc^2$, indicates that energy and mass are actually two sides of the same thing.

Ancient Great Rishis (Sages) discovered how the world was created by a non-manifested state of pure consciousness. From this state of absolute consciousness emerged the first sound vibration, the soundless Aum. The first space, or ether, elements were created from this vibration. Ether began to move and the movement created air and the movement of friction was heat-shaped light, which then produced the fire element. From the fire's heat dissolved some parts of the ether to a liquid form and so the water element was created. When the water became fixed in form then it became earth element molecules. From a different point of view: protons, neutrons, electrons, and other subatomic particles in the atom represent the earth element. The energies of that atom, which keeps the electrons around the nucleus, represent the water element. When the atom exploded and released colossal energy, the fire element came into being. The force that gets electrons moving around the nucleus represents the air element. The space in which they move represents the space element. In other words, all five elements are everywhere in all forms of matter.

In Vedic tradition, the five elements are called *Panchabhutas*, which connect the person in a Vastu home with the beneficial earth and cosmic energies from the sun. These elements of earth, water, fire, air, and space are each connected with a particular direction which acknowledges the basic laws of nature. By honoring these elements and their energies, we become more aligned with nature and therefore can achieve greater harmony in our everyday lives.

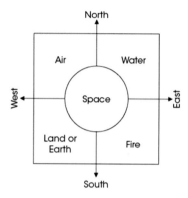

The earth element is represented by plants, trees, rocks, soil, and mountains, and is therefore a solid, dense, and grounded element. People need a solid foundation to survive in this physical world. The earth element is linked to the southwest direction and is the best choice for the location of a master bedroom. The element of earth is associated with earth-toned colors (all shades of brown). These colors would be earth-colored pigments of brown, sepia, sienna, ochre, umber, and cinnamon.

In Vedic tradition, water is commonly used as a metaphor for pure consciousness. As the northeast is where the energy waves of the water elements collect, the best place to locate indoor and outdoor water features (pools, ponds, waterfalls, fountains, and aquariums) would be in this region of the home and yard. The element of water is associated with green or green-blues. You can honor this element by using green-toned paints, actual water features, or pictures of water.

The southeast is dominated by the fire element and is the best place for fireplaces, kitchens, and electrical devices. To honor this element, light a fire either in a fireplace or by using non-toxic beeswax candles. The element of fire is acknowledged by intense golden-orange, gold, golden-yellow and red shades, with red being the core color. A kitchen painted in an apricot tone would not only honor the fire energies, but would also be energizing to the person that performed cooking chores in this room.

Movement is normally associated with the element of air which is liveliest in the northwest. To keep the air in your home fresh, open windows and use fans and air purifiers in the northwest corners of your rooms. Wind chimes, mobiles, and wind streamers are best placed in the northwest areas. To get the most benefit from the prana (life-force energy) in the air, learn and practice yoga breathing techniques, called *pranayama* (which will be discussed in greater detail in chapter 7). Guestrooms are normally best located in this area of the home as well. The element of air is normally portrayed as blue. This color and the many shades it comes in resonate with the qualities of air.

The element of space is linked to sound and silence. This element is represented by the center of a building and the center of each individual room and is an element of energetic and dynamic space. It is the connection between the seen and the unseen. This element is honored by keeping the center of each room clean and clear of objects. To keep reverence of this open space, heavy objects are never placed in the center of the room. The element of space, which is the center of the Vastu Purusha Mandala, or the universe in miniature, is such a subtle and expansive element that no particular color has been assigned to it formally. It is usually represented by the color white which is viewed as pure.

Shiva and Shakti

Besides the five elements, we should also consider the effects of the prana flow from the sun and the moon. Shiva (the Sun) is represented by the direction of east because this is where the sun rises. Shiva is the Divine Father, the male positive prana, or life force energy. Vastu principles say it is important to have more windows and doors in the east because it is important for the first ultraviolet sun rays to enter the home and nourish the people living there. Those first rays of the sun are very important for the cells of our body to be recharged. We carry this prana with us throughout the day to make us more productive, successful, and to ultimately achieve wealth. The north is represented by Shakti (the Moon), who is the Divine Mother and positive female aspect of cosmic energy. Shakti represents creativity, health, wealth, and love. Openings like windows and doors in the north are beneficial.

Areas of the northeast represent the combination of Shiva and Shakti and are a very important part of the home. According to Indian mythology, both Shiva and Shakti are positive and equal to each other and cannot function without each other. There must always be balance in creation so the male and female principles can exist in harmony. If Shiva (the male) is dominating too much, with lack of Shakti, the effect can be tough, hard, or even cruel. One becomes materialistic with no inner guidance and will do anything to get more power and will not care for others. If Shakti (the female) is dominating, without Shiva, the inspirations and ideas and inner guidance that she provides will never manifest in the material world. Both are needed and balance is very important if one wants to get health, wealth, and have good relationships.

When the energies of Shiva and Shakti enter a home, they should flow slowly throughout the home and be encouraged to stay as long as possible. They should be able to enter from the northeast, north, and east and slowly exit through the southwest, south, or west regions of the home. Their flow should always be in balance and is essential for a harmonious home.

Colors

The use of colors to create environments that are uplifting, encouraging, and relaxing is an ancient art of its own. You may need to experiment with different shades and hues to determine which colors will provide the best results for you and your family. Color has an emotional impact that is very individualized. Every color has the ability to affect us energetically with a unique vibrational rate that can be not only pleasurable, but also nourishing to the body. Colors are food for your mental, physical, and spiritual health.

Below is a list of Vastu colors and the energy they represent:

- **Red:** Fire, blood, love, passion, sexuality, courage, strength, drama, the creative force, anger, war, danger, sacrifice, frustration
- **Orange:** Health, vitality, enthusiasm, optimism, development, confidence, socialization
- **Yellow:** Joy, happiness, attention, creativity
- **Green:** Growth, cure, healing, renewal, abundance, prosperity, peace, joy, cooperation, harmony—A good Vastu color
- **Blue:** Calm, integrity, inspiration, stability, withdraw, loneliness
- **Purple:** Mystery, authority, luxury, spiritual wealth, meditation
- **White:** Life and death, innocence, purity, hygiene
- **Pink:** Romance and love, peace, proximity, cooperation, harmony, relaxation, happy mood.
- **Black:** Calm, grief, mystery, magic, elegant, hot, depression
- **Brown:** Stability, safety, security, roots, fidelity
- **Gray:** Compromise, resting, self-control, self-criticism

Remember to take a look at the natural colors available in the world outside of your home and try to incorporate those same colors within your living environment to reap the best results of connecting with the earth, its energies, and the spiritual nature of all creation. Better yet, bring live plants, flowers, leaves, twigs and rocks into your home to add to the vitality of your home. Even the colors that you choose to adorn your body with will have a healing and nourishing effect on your overall health.

Chapter 3: Bedrooms

As the northeast region is considered sacred to religious/spiritual practices like meditation and yoga, and the southeast is considered an area ruled by fire, it is never advisable to have a bedroom in either area. If you must have a bedroom in the southeast, do not place your bed in the southeast corner of the room. Instead, sleep with your head to the south and your feet to the north to lessen the effect of sleeping in a fire region. The way prana flows, it is good to avoid placing beds in the center of the room. Sleeping with your head to the south is believed to bring deep sleep and grants a longer life to the occupants of the room, while sleeping with your head to the east is believed to bring enlightenment and knowledge. Sleeping with your head to the east or south also promotes healing. Avoid sleeping with your head towards the north. Sleeping with your head in the north is not good for your health and does not allow for a restful sleep due to magnetic polar energies. There should never be windows behind your head when you are sleeping.

The walls should be different shades of blue, green, rose, or other earth-toned colors to encourage good sleep. Pictures or wall hangings that relate to nature, that are pretty to look at and bring you joy, should be placed in such a way that you see them every day when you first wake up. Curtains should be of a light neutral color and lightweight material.

Mirrors should not be in your bedroom as they disturb sleep, can cause restless sleep, and have caused strange dreams to the occupants of the room. If it is necessary to have a mirror in your bedroom, it should not show a reflection of the bed.

Most bedrooms contain a few large pieces of furniture. These heavy items should be placed in the south, southwestern, or west areas of the room. Furniture should not be placed in direct contact with the walls. The center of the room should be kept clear of all obstacles, including furniture, toys, and clutter.

There should be no religious pictures or shrines in your bedroom. These are better placed in an area of your home devoted to religious practices. Placing them in a bedroom can generate too much energy and make sleeping difficult. The same holds true for pictures of children, parents, and other relatives.

There should be no television in your bedroom as the electrical radiation and the stimulation that occurs from viewing the television do not lead to restfulness. The bedroom should be a place of serene private space to which you can retreat for peaceful sleep, relaxation, and intimacy. It should also be a work-free zone so that your mind and body can rest and settle down to a less busy energy level. If you find you must place a computer in your bedroom for lack of space to put it anywhere else in the house, find a way to partition it off or cover it up when it is not in use. In this way, you will honor the need to separate the energies of work and relaxation and allow for better sleeping conditions.

Vastu principles warn against using metal for beds since metal complicates electromagnetic fields that could affect your health and may affect your ability to have a good night's sleep. It is recommended to use a wooden bed or other natural material such as rattan or bamboo. Headboards are recommended as they provide metaphorical support while footboards create a feeling of being restricted and can leave you feeling boxed in. Natural fibers for your bed and linens are healthy and can prevent allergic reactions; consider items made from cotton, silk, wool, hemp, flax, beech wood, cellulose, linen, natural rubber, and wool. If you experience difficulty sleeping, fresh bedding can provide a sense of well-being and relaxation that are conductive to healthier sleep habits.

Overhead beams are common decorative structural designs in homes that are not beneficial to sleep beneath as they disrupt the natural flows of energy in a room. If there is one over your bed, it is advisable to add a canopy or hang fabric above the bed to protect yourself from these oppressive energy patterns.

Bathroom doors attached to bedrooms should always remain closed. Besides the cleanliness issue, the water elements contained in a bathroom will have an effect on the energy flowing in your bedroom if the door remains open for any length of time.

Master Bedrooms

The ideal location for a master bedroom is in the south or southwestern corner of the house. The master bedroom should always be bigger than all other bedrooms in a home. If a home has multiple floors, the master bedroom should be on the top floor.

It is fine to have happy pictures of yourself and your partner or other divine couples, as this will create a positive effect on the room.

In order to keep a well-balanced energy within the master bedroom, there should be an equal amount of matching items on both sides of the bed. If there is a lamp on one night stand, there should also be a lamp on the other night stand. Closet space and dresser drawer space should be equally divided. There should always be an equal amount of pillows on the bed. This balance is important to the relationship of the people that share the bedroom. Neither gender should dominate the room, thereby making each feel invited and welcomed within the bedroom.

Children's Bedrooms

A child's room is not that much different than an adult's room except that it is also normally their play and study area as well as a sleeping area. It still needs to be a relaxing haven to which they can retreat for privacy. Therefore, more attention to detail is needed to keep the natural flow of energies going in a correct order so as to keep the child from becoming stubborn and agitated when the natural flow is disrupted. Proper alignment of items in their rooms can lead to better concentration, better mental attitudes, and even better health.

The west side of the house is best for young children. A bedroom in the east area of the home is ideal for teenage children.

It is common practice in today's society for children to complete school work and play computer games in their bedrooms as well as watch television. If these types of electronic devices are to be allowed in the bedroom, the best possible placement for them would be to put the computer on the north side of the room and the television on the southeastern side of the room. This, at least, evens out the electronic interference that can occur with the natural energies of the earth.

Tables or desks designed for study should be placed so they face east. The study area should be kept free of clutter in order to help children concentrate on their studies and remain focused. While this area may require additional lighting, be aware that harsh unnatural lighting will cause strain and lack of focus. Lamps with sharp angles and edges will increase stress in this area. It is suggested that smooth-shaped lamps with light-colored shades be used with full spectrum light bulbs.

Guest Bedrooms

The guest bedroom is an important room in your house as you want your visitors to feel invited and comforted, yet you do not wish them to overstay their welcome and become dominating figures within your household. You want your visitors to feel positive energy no matter what their cultural beliefs may be and you want to be able to eradicate any negative energies they may bring into your household, whether they mean to or not.

A bedroom in the northwest is the best location for a guest room, with the bed placed in the southwestern part of the room. Guests placed in rooms in the southeast will have a difficult time sleeping and will become disagreeable and bring disharmony to your household.

Chapter 4: Other Rooms and Areas of the Home

Living Room

The living room (also called the drawing room) is an area of your home that you will spend a lot of your time in with your family and guests. This room must bring us comfort and peace in order to keep harmony in our lives and the lives of the people we interact with within this room. This room has the ability to affect your life in many ways and is therefore very important to be as close to Vastu Shastra guidelines as possible.

The location of a living room within your home influences the types of activities that will have the greatest success. Because I am focusing on homes that are already built, you can use the following information to determine which activities are best suited for your living room and how to improve upon the energies of your specific room's location. Generally, the best location for a living room is in the east, north, or west areas of a home.

There are several tips for the items within the room that should be followed as closely as possible for the best results in tuning into the natural energy flows of nature. Incorporating as many of these changes into your home will allow you to feel better physically, mentally, and spiritually.

Wall colors should be white or light shades of green. These colors will create a sense of togetherness and affection for the people in the room. Light shades of yellow and blue are also acceptable. If you have windows or doors on the north and east walls, use only light curtains. If you have windows or doors on the south and west walls, use heavy curtains in these areas. The use of the colors red and black are never recommended for the living room space.

Because the northeast area is considered a sacred area, keep this area free of clutter and clean. It is suggested that live plants be placed in this area to encourage tranquility and peace within the room. It is recommended that you never display artificial or plastic flowers. Dried flowers attract negative energy because they represent either autumn or dead energy and provide no prana. Cactus plants are not recommended to have in your home. Beautiful pictures of nature and other nice harmonious art works would be best suited for this area.

Avoid having pictures that can disturb the peace of the room especially if they depict war, death, pain, horrors, and even deceased people. Not only would this give the room a gloomy and unwelcoming feeling, it would also add negative energy to the household. The living room does not need mirrors to distract people from the art of living in the moment. Try to avoid hanging mirrors or reflective items that could be used as a mirrored surface in the living room area.

Large electronic equipment pieces, such as a television, should be placed in the southeast corner of the room. If the room has a fireplace, this would also be the ideal location for it.

The living room should ideally be brightly lit with a natural light source if possible. Living rooms in the east and north sections of the home with the ability to have natural morning sunlight will benefit from additional positive energy vibrations.

Furniture in the living room should be square or rectangular in shape. Objects with sharp points, uneven sides, circular or oval, hexagonal or octagonal, or other odd sizes can create a disruption in the natural flow of energy and therefore have a negative effect on the occupants of the room as well as the rest of the home. Heavy furniture items should be located primarily in the west, south, or southwestern areas of the room.

Kitchen

This room is a hot spot of all kinds of energies, both natural and manmade. While it is dictated by the Vastu Shastra that a kitchen be located in the southeast quadrant of your home, there are still a few things you can do if this is not where your kitchen is located.

Do not use microwave ovens. Microwave ovens destroy the beneficial balance of nature in foods and make them into something that does not nourish the body. Convection ovens work just as well when creating healthy food and are less drying to the foods you are preparing.

It is very important for natural sunlight to enter the kitchen if possible. The wall colors should be very light shades of yellow, orange, or white. In fact, all items in this room should be light and bright in color. Dark colors in a kitchen are not recommended.

The kitchen should always be kept clean and uncluttered. Items should be used, cleaned, and returned to their proper storage spot as quickly as possible. This practice is not only for health and safety reasons, but it also creates a positive energy flow within the room.

Dining Room

The dining room has the benefit of allowing the family to gather together to share life events and build family harmony. A well laid-out room will increase the prosperity of all family members. An attractive setting in which you can relax, with unchipped dishes and silverware that fits your hand properly, will go a long ways towards creating a positive atmosphere within your home.

Food is often taken for granted and thereby not given the honor it deserves considering we could not survive without it. India has on old saying: "Food is Brahman." This means food is the divine wholeness that is bestowed upon you. The dining room gives us the opportunity to honor this divine wholeness by reminding us to slow down and enjoy the experience of eating.

Many people have dishes and silverware that is only used for special occasions. Each meal should be a special occasion where you honor the fact that you have food to eat. Research has shown that eating from silver utensils instead of the standard steel silverware actually is healthier for a person. So use your good dishes for dining, not just for display. You and your family will feel better after each meal.

While the color of this room could be any color, depending on direction and element color, besides red or black, the shades should be kept to subdued qualities so as to not be overpowering when meals are served and people are trying to relax. Neutral shades work best.

Dining areas should be located in the east or west quadrants of a home to receive the benefits of natural lighting. If located on the east side of a home, a family can receive the first rays of the morning sunrise which are described to be very beneficial to the health of all people. Ideally, it should be located close to the kitchen for ease of serving prepared food.

If you place a cupboard in this room for storage of dishes and utensils, it should be located in the southwestern quadrant of the room.

Office or Study Room

The office or study is most often used as a room for learning, where a person requires peace and quiet so they can concentrate on studies or work. By following Vastu Shastra principles for the layout and location of this room, the vibrations of this room, which creates unseen noises, will be lessened and will allow the room to provide you with peace, knowledge, and even comfort.

This room would be best located on the east or west side of the home. Having this room in the southern regions of the home can lead to distractions that will make study almost impossible. The occupant of the room should always face north or east while they undertake the task of learning.

Light neutral colors have been proven to help with the learning process. Therefore, the entire room should be a balance of yellows, which are good for learning, and earth colors, which are good for grounding and focusing.

Natural lighting would be the best lighting but may not be bright enough. If a table lamp is used, the use of full spectrum bulbs is strongly encouraged as they are the closest to natural sunlight.

The study desk or table should be square or rectangular in shape and large enough in size to accommodate the work you will be doing on a regular basis. A desk that is too small will stifle creativity and affect a person's ability to focus. A desk that is too large will feel overwhelming and could become a distraction to the user. The study desk should never be placed in a corner or touching a wall, nor should it face a window or blank wall. It should also never be placed in the direct center of the room. It is also not advised to sit with your back to a window.

Bookshelves should be on the southern or western walls but should never be directly over the study table or desk area.

Be sure that windows do not cause a glare on the screen causing undue eye strain.

Mirrors should not be hung in a study room as they prove to be too much of a distraction. If wall hangings are used, they should depict scenes of peaceful gardens and trees.

Bathrooms

Bathrooms should always feel clean, bright, fresh, airy, and light. Bathrooms and toilets have always had a bad history of disease and other health issues. In the past, bathrooms and toilets were not part of the home—they were normally outside in the yard—and in those days it was considered unhealthy and unclean. Today we have modern bathrooms and toilets which should be kept clean and the lid of the toilet should be closed when not in use. Bathroom doors should always be closed.

The best location for a bathroom is in the northwest. No matter where your bathroom is located, if it has a window, open it and allow the outside air to help keep this room feeling fresh. If you have no windows, consider the use of incense, oil diffusers, plug-in air purifiers, bright lighting, and live plants. Live plants in your bathroom can help correct poor energy flows and create a positive boost to your room. They help eliminate odors and provide oxygen while providing a direct connection to nature.

Bathroom colors should be bright, inviting, cheerful, yet soothing. Depending on whether you have a good natural light source, softer colors can be used if you do, brighter colors should be used if you are lacking in light. Never use black or red in your bathroom.

Main Entranceways

Vastu Shastra standards talk about the major importance of the front entrance ways or doorways of a house. This is where the positive prana energies and vibrations enter your home. This entrance area is the doorway to wealth and you should strive to make it look that way. This area should always be welcoming as it is a representation of the rest of your home.

A front door that opens inwards is welcoming, as it signifies a pulling in of the prana, instead of pushing the prana energies away. If there is a wall in front of the door, there should be no mirrors or other reflective items hung on that wall.

Stairs

While there is little that can be done for stairways that have been built outside of the Vastu Shastra guidelines, I will include a few points to remember in case you decide to remodel or repair stairs that already exist.

The color of stairs and the walls around them should always be light in color and shades. Never use dark colors on a staircase.

Any stairs that require repair must be attended to immediately. Besides the fact that injuries may occur, unrepaired stairways lead to tension in a household.

Space under stairways should never be used as living areas in a home. The space under stairways should only be used for storage.

Basements

While Vastu Shastra does not consider it wise to use or even have vacant space under your dwelling, it has become common practice for people to construct basements due to limited space in most residences. Basements should never be used for residential living purposes; it is best used for storage. It is believed that this practice is understood to mean that people are not intended to live beneath the ground as energy flows above the ground and would therefore be disrupted or negative for the person(s) living in a basement arrangement.

Space should remain open in the northern and eastern portions of the basement with heavy items being placed in the southern and western quadrants.

Basements should be painted in light soothing colors that bring light into the space. Never use dark colors that will leave dark areas or shadows. Make sure the area has bright lighting available if no windows are present.

Chapter 5: Cleaning to Improve Vastu Energies

Ancient Vedic perspective teaches that physical congestion not only affects the serenity of your home, it can also affect you in physical, mental, emotional, and spiritual ways. Clutter in your physical environment can cause stress, create health issues, and does nothing to help your ability to think and act clearly. To enhance success in your life and create a peaceful and orderly environment, you must clear the clutter from your home. Clutter can be any physical item that is not needed or items that are left unorganized.

Research published in the field of neuroscience has concluded that clearing clutter from your home and work environments will allow you to process information and focus effectively. This research also proved that organizing your home and having an uncluttered environment means you will be distracted less often, be more productive, and feel less irritability.

According to Vastu Shastra standards, which is the science of environmental harmony, when clutter causes stress it also causes a reduction and restriction in the life force energies. Depending on where the clutter is located within your home, it can have very specific impacts on your life. For example:

- Clutter in the northwest affects all your relationships and stability of the mind.
- Clutter in the northeast blocks your future advancements, both spiritually and financially.
- Clutter in the southeast affects your health and productivity. It will also affect areas of passion, creativity, as well as your physical energy.
- Clutter in the southwest affects areas of support, which includes your skeletal bone structure (which can show up as back pain) and your career.

Because clutter has such a huge impact on so many areas of our lives, it is very important to dispose of items that are old and no longer needed or do not reflect who you are. Cleaning clutter will help you create a better flow of energy in your home, help you to feel more productive, and will leave you feeling less stressed. It will also simplify your life, give you more physical space in your home, and open your emotions for new possibilities so you can thrive.

The best way to start the process is to start small. Try cleaning out a drawer. Set a time limit to help you stay focused on the task so you won't become overwhelmed. Use the following steps to guide you through the process:

1. Take everything out of the drawer
2. Create three plies:
   - The first pile is the giveaway pile
   - The second pile is the throw away pile
   - The last pile is what you will keep (Make sure you keep only what you need.)
3. Place your kept items back in the drawer. Be sure to keep it organized.

Now take a short break and evaluate how you feel inside. To settle your mind, place your hand over your heart and take a few deep breaths in through the nose and out through the mouth. You should be able to feel a subtle energetic effect. When you're ready, you can move on to the next area that needs to be decluttered and on to larger projects or areas of your home.

Remember that cleaning the clutter has to be maintained. Everything has a proper place and clutter should be controlled to keep stress out of your environment.

Once the clutter is removed from your home, a further step can be taken to align the energies of your home. The art of cleaning, balancing, and enhancing the energetic levels of your home is known as space clearing. Space clearing helps us keep the flow of energy around us clean and clear by removing obstacles and restoring balance and harmony. It has been reported that after a space cleaning has been completed, occupants of the home usually feel more confident, have more energy, feel more positive, and report more clarity in their daily lives.

A space clearing is something you will want to do initially after you have cleaned and removed unwanted clutter from your home, and then at least once a month thereafter or any time a major life changing event occurs. The process is quite simple and easy to complete. It does require a good quality bell (brass or Tibetan bells work well), an incense stick holder, and good quality incense sticks. The recommended times to do this are early in the morning or at sunset.

Follow these steps to complete a space clearing in your home:

1. After all the clutter has been removed and your home is clean, open all the doors and windows. Also open all cupboards and drawers.
2. Turn on all your lights and any fans that you have in the home.
3. Turn on some soft music. (Meditation or yoga style music is best)
4. Walk through your home with a burning incense stick and ring the bell in every corner of every room.

The entire process should only take a few minutes to complete depending on the size of your home. Once you have finished the above steps, you can close your doors and windows, close your cupboards and drawers, turn off unneeded lights and fans, and either continue to find peace with your music choice or turn it off as well. You should find that your home feels much more peaceful and relaxing.

Chapter 6:
The Yard and Garden

Vastu Shastra principles provide guidance for planning outdoor spaces whether it is a garden, trees, plants, or general landscaping. These guidelines were provided so people would be in balance with nature and reap the benefits of good health, peace, positivity, and harmony in their lives.

We already know that plants provide the oxygen that we need to survive. They also purify the air we breathe and provide shade and beauty for us to enjoy. Vastu gardens honor nature by working with it.

Like Vastu guidelines for inside your home, the same basic principles apply to your yard. Heavier items like stone sculptures, rock gardens, green houses, potting sheds, and other storage areas are best located in the southwestern regions of your yard. The south and west are also the best place to plant tall trees for the shade they will provide from the hottest part of the day.

If you use metal in your garden, such as garden tools, the use of copper is recommended as it heals the soil instead of drying it out. Using natural remedies for disease and insect issues also helps your garden to remain in tune with nature. There are numerous books and local nurseries that can help you use organic measures instead of chemicals in your yard and garden.

To achieve the best energetic effects from your yard and garden efforts, use natural materials like stone, wood, rock, and bamboo. While concrete blocks may save you time and effort, they can block some of the positive earth prana and create a sterile environment.

Outdoor water features have the ability to provide a soothing influence. As water represents the flow of abundance, having water features are not only beautiful to look at, they may also create an atmosphere of prosperity and wealth. Adding water lotuses for their beauty has the added benefit of the symbolic representation of abundance and spiritual perfection. Check with your local nursery to see what varieties will work in your geographical area and what type of seasonal care they may require.

Always place ponds, fountains, and waterfalls in the northeast or north areas of your yard. This is regarded as a sacred zone and should be kept clean, orderly, and pure at all times. Healing herbs would be a wonderful addition to this area of your yard. Never allow trash or gardening sheds to be placed in this area of your yard. Fruit-bearing trees are also known to provide additional healing prana when planted in this area.

Because the northwest is dedicated to the element of air, this is the best yard location for wind streamers, wind chimes, mobiles, swings, and any other items that react to wind flow. Even plants that are meant to sway in the wind would be a good addition to this location. Remember not to place large items in this area that would restrict air flow as this region is meant to have free flowing air all of the time.

The fire element rules the southeast and should be where you place grills, fireplaces, fire pits, outdoor kitchens, or other fire items. When you are using this area you could light candles to encourage the flow of prana. It would also be beneficial to add fiery-colored plants and flowers to this area that suggest red and golden flames.

Your yard and garden should be a reflection of your personality. The colors and items that you add to your yard will increase your energy levels if they are pleasing to you and will be even more beneficial if they follow the basic guidelines of Vastu principles. Grapes will remind you of abundance, sweetly scented flowers tend to bring spiritual reminders, and a multitude of colors remind us of the many varieties in life. Go with what brings you joy.

Chapter 7: Improve and Increase Personal Prana

As I described before, prana is the subtle universal life force energy that is essential to every living creature. We use it on a daily basis and therefore should be just as aware of our own energy forces as we are about the energies in our environment. If we spend the time to improve the homes we live in, it is just as important to spend time making sure that our own energy levels are positive, balanced and in harmony with nature so that we can reap the full benefits of living by Vastu Shastra standards and achieve lives that are healthy, wealthy, and peaceful.

To take a look at our own prana, we must take the time to invest in our personal habits of rest and relaxation. Just as our homes can become filled with chaos and clutter, so too can our minds and spirit become overwhelmed with the stresses brought on by the chores of everyday life. In order to feel the full benefits of a home that is modified to Vastu Shastra standards, a person must also be able to calm the mind and spirit to feel the peacefulness and harmony that nature can provide.

While there are many methods available to help a person achieve this inner peace and harmony, many of us find it difficult to incorporate a routine into our lives that allow us to maintain these feelings for any length of time. We tend to spend our lives bouncing from one crisis to another and wonder why we feel stress and unhappiness. The good news is that there is a way to add simple routines into your daily schedule that are easy to follow, do not require expensive equipment or gadgets, and will not take up long periods of time, which is what stops most of us from following through with what we know is good for us no matter how badly we want to change things in our lives. Although I will give you a few tips here, feel free to expand your search for areas that fit with your life style that you find comfort in and will stick with in the long run.

Pranayama, a common form of breathing taught frequently with yoga classes, has been interpreted to mean "control of breath." While there are numerous variations of Pranayama, I will give you an example of a method that is commonly used:

Nadi Shodhana Pranayama (also known as Anulom Vilom Pranayama) is an alternate nostril breathing technique. This technique helps balance the inner Shiva and Shakti prana which helps to calm the mind, is good for your health, and brings happiness and peacefulness. It helps relieve tension and fatigue by clearing blocked energy channels in the body.

To do Nadi Shodhana Pranayama, sit in a comfortable position with your spine erect and your shoulders relaxed. Put your left hand on your left knee with your palm open and facing upwards. With your right hand, put the tip of your index finger and middle finger between your eyebrows (gently resting in this area with no pressure), with your ring finger and little finger on the left side of your nose and your thumb on the right side of your nose. You will use the ring finger and little finger to close (or open) the left nostril while the thumb will be used to close (or open) the right nostril. Start by taking a normal breath, in and out, to relax yourself and begin the process of Nadi Shodhana breathing. When you are ready to begin, gently push your thumb down on the right nostril and breathe in through the left nostril. Push the left nostril closed, open the right nostril, and breathe out from the right nostril. (Your exhales should be longer than your inhales, possibly a count of 4 for inhalations and 6 for exhalations). Breathe in through the right nostril, close the right nostril, open the left nostril, and exhale out through the left side. You have now completed one round. Continue this pattern for a total of 10 rounds, always breathing through the nose, not the mouth, keeping your eyes closed during the process. Remember to take deep, long, smooth breaths without using force or effort. Because this breathing exercise is an excellent way to center the mind and find calmness, it is a great time to follow up with other meditative exercises.

There are numerous meditation techniques available from visualization routines to the use of music and sounds. Even lighting a candle and simply staring into the flame for a few minutes and focusing on nothing but the flicker of that flame can be used as a short form of meditation. The goal of any short meditation process is to give your mind a break and help you find your inner peace. You are encouraged to find a style that works for you and use it regularly. Meditation is the most common form of relaxation that helps to bring balance and inner peace. Meditation not only helps to calm the mind, it also provides numerous other health benefits such as lowering blood pressure, reducing stress and anxiety, encouraging better sleep, regulating mood, and increasing creativity. All of these benefits will enhance the prana in your life and home.

Most people immediately create an image in their mind of a person sitting with crossed legs, eyes closed, and chanting "ohm" for long periods of time. While this can be true for some, this is not the only way to meditate and you should not let this preconceived idea stop you from trying a simpler version of meditation that may work better for you to start with. Short meditations can last anywhere from one to five minutes and can be done anywhere you are comfortable. For more information about meditation, you should acquire a copy of: *Meditation for Beginners: The Ultimate and Easy Guide to Learn How to Be Peaceful and Relieve Stress, Anxiety, and Depression*, or seek out help from a class on meditation in an area close to you. There are many teachers that can help you with techniques and provide additional tips and information about meditation that I do not have the ability to provide in detail in this book.

There are also many forms of gentle exercises that can be used to get your mind into a more focused and relaxed state that each has benefits of their own. Although I will not get into each of them individually, I will give you this brief list to consider:

- **Yoga:** Uses stretching, enhanced breath control, and the strengthening of core muscles. Promotes mental, physical, and spiritual awareness.
- **Qigong:** Gentle, focused movements that lead to a calmer sense of overall well-being.
- **Pilates:** A physical fitness system which encourages mind focus and aids in calming the mind.
- **Tai Chi:** Some of its forms with slow movements and monitored breathing techniques teaches mind and body control.

Any form of exercise or training that encourages muscle movements and breathing control is beneficial to help slow the mind down.

There may also be spiritual routines that you have that can help you in your quest for serenity and peacefulness. Every culture and belief system has its own areas of expertise in the field of spiritual cleansing. If you have a firm belief in one of these systems, be sure to incorporate it into your daily life.

It is important to remember that your body is a temple in its own way. So like your home, it must be taken care of to ensure balance and harmony. Nutrition plays a role in this process too. You should be aware of the quality of the food that you ingest to ensure that you are taking in the proper foods that will keep you healthy and vigorous. A healthy body means you will have the capacity to make healthy choices in all areas of your life.

For thousands of years now, the people in India have used the tradition of Vastu to support their relationships, finances, and health. Vastu is considered a sister tradition of Ayurveda (the ancient healing system of India). Patients are often given Vastu suggestions for their homes as part of a holistic treatment plan for their personal health.

The same five elements that Vastu homes are designed to be in harmony with also influence the body and a person's health and quality of life. Ayurveda teaches that the air element affects the nervous system and the mind. The water element is represented by the reproductive system, the urinary system, and the lymphatic systems. The fire element is associated with your digestive system and energy levels. Earth element is linked to the lower back. By honoring these elements in our homes, we can honor them in our bodies as well.

By ensuring that your home and personal prana are in tune with the universal flows of energies that surround you every minute of every day, you will find that peacefulness and tranquility are a normal part of your existence. When balance is achieved, your life will feel new and exciting.

Conclusion

Vastu is relatively new in the Western culture. Yoga and Ayurveda treats the body and mind that is associated with the environment at the quantum level. When we begin to change the interior like the exterior, we also individually change automatically to achieve a more sustainable balance in life. The Chinese Feng Shui is already very famous and has opened the way for the Indian Vastu Shastra.

We all want good fortune, health, wealth, happiness, and overall success. Vastu increases positive energy forces within your home and work spaces to help you achieve permanent changes in your life and well-being. Even simply rearranging objects in a room can create a new set of vibrations and Vastu knowledge helps to assure that those vibrations will enhance your life. When properly applied, Vastu methodology will bring out the best from your living environment and promises you a better future.

For a deeper or tailor-made analysis, it is strongly recommended that you seek out expert advice from a Vastu professional. A professional in the Vastu field can provide additional information and remedies for your home, as well as provide guidance if you are planning on building or adding onto your current home structure. A professional can address changes that will improve your current situation and offer suggestions for changes that will improve your overall health and well-being, as well as offer guidance for structural designs that follow Vastu Shastra standards.

I hope this book was able to help you get a brief overview about the basic knowledge of Vastu standards and methodology. Although the topic is diverse and it is impossible to cover all of it in such a short literary work, I have tried to condense the most useful knowledge for you, my readers, so that you can take this book as your first step towards Vastu standards. The information has been arranged in such a way that all readers can understand it in the easiest terms. All the terminology used in the book, which may seem uncomfortable for the untrained reader, has been explained in detail which I hope has been helpful.

Finally, if you enjoyed this book, then I'd like to ask you for a favor. Would you be kind enough to leave a review for this book on Amazon? It'd be greatly appreciated!

Thank you and good luck!

Michael Dinuri
www.dinuri.com

About the Author

Michael Dinuri is a Swedish Ayurveda, yoga, and Vaastu practitioner and author. Dinuri has always believed that life has unlimited possibilities to offer and he is passionate about helping other people change their lives and share his knowledge. As a result, he is now able to professionally work with personal development and wellness.

Dinuri's grandparents originated from northwest India, a country where yoga and alternative medicine has been used since ancient times and is still commonly used in everyday life. At an early age, encouraged and inspired by his paternal grandmother, he became intrigued by the infinite ancient knowledge and wisdom of human life and nature.

A lot of Dinuri's knowledge has been obtained through the studies of ancient scriptures and by being a disciple of well-known teachers and masters of India and other parts of the world. Dinuri also has a vast interest in mysticism and has a passion for fulfilling everyone's potential as a human being.

"The key to the road of happiness is to learn how to understand our inner being, and in doing so, be able to enjoy our every moment to the fullest."

— Michael Dinuri

Other Books by Michael Dinuri:

Meditation for Beginners
The Ultimate and Easy Guide to Learn How to Be Peaceful and Relieve Stress, Anxiety And Depression

Meditation is a lifestyle skill that brings not only peacefulness to the person practicing the skill, but also provides lifelong health benefits that add longevity and quality of life. It is a simple skill that can be practiced by anyone of any age, race, religion, political view point, or regional location with no special requirements or equipment needed.

This book will cover not only the benefits from a regular meditation schedule, but will also provide tips for short, easy to use, mini meditations for those on-the-go days when you just need a break from the harsh realities of everyday living

Ayurveda Weight Loss
Successful 10-Day Ayurvedic Detox Diet And Weight Loss Program

Lose Weight Permanently with Ayurveda and Maintain It!

The ayurvedic way of treatment can undoubtedly help in fighting against excess body fat and toxic substances. With the help of an ayurvedic detox program, the body can get rid of various health problems especially from excess fat. A 10-day ayurvedic diet program will help you get rid of excess body fat without any trouble. Using an ayurvedic way of treatment, body weight can be lost by fast and gradual ways, and thus you will not need to worry about your excess weight. Ayurveda has a complete set of solutions for every kind of weight problem you have.

Made in the USA
Lexington, KY
14 May 2018